THE CAMBRIDGE MISCELLANY

IX

HORACE

The Lewis Fry Memorial Lectures
University of Bristol, 1932

HORACE

A Return to Allegiance

By

T. R. GLOVER

*Ridentem dicere verum
Quid vetat?*

CAMBRIDGE
AT THE UNIVERSITY PRESS
1932

CAMBRIDGE UNIVERSITY PRESS
Cambridge, New York, Melbourne, Madrid, Cape Town,
Singapore, São Paulo, Delhi, Tokyo, Mexico City

Cambridge University Press
The Edinburgh Building, Cambridge CB2 8RU, UK

Published in the United States of America by Cambridge University Press, New York

www.cambridge.org
Information on this title: www.cambridge.org/9781107670402

© Cambridge University Press 1932

First published 1932
First paperback edition 2011

A catalogue record for this publication is available from the British Library

ISBN 978-1-107-67040-2 Paperback

To

THE TWO BRISTOLIANS
WHOM I LIKE THE BEST

PREFACE

The invitation to deliver the Lewis Fry Memorial Lectures in the University of Bristol came to me as a surprise, but a welcome one. I am "a citizen of no mean city"; and such a call from my city could not fail to bring pleasure. The name of the foundation itself recalled old memories. The earliest political event I remember was the election of Lewis Fry as Member of Parliament for Bristol in 1878. He and his colleague, Samuel Morley, gave "Members' Scholarships" at the Bristol Grammar School, one of which fell to my lot in the days when I first was reading Horace; and here, after nearly half a century, I was again to be brought into pleasant contact with the name of Lewis Fry.

I was to address myself, I was told, to the University, not to a mere group of students specializing in one line of study. Then my subject? I had to decide that. But I sought advice, and proposed two themes. One was the romantic story of my other home in Canada, a city on lake and river made famous under three names, the Cataraqui of the Indians, the Fort Frontenac of the French, the Kingston of the United Empire Loyalists. The other proposal was Horace, and for Horace all my friends gave their votes, perhaps because he was more familiar to them.

But I was further told, you must not be too technical; you must not quote too much Latin; this is a modern University. With what success I have obeyed my instructions, or whether they quite precluded the success he would have wished, the reader must judge. But whatever listeners and readers may say, let me confess that the writer enjoyed his task. And after that there is no more for me to say, unless to explain that the Latin in the text is there for the reader's delight; it was not inflicted on the listeners; and if the reader "wants it translated", let him look again and he will find that he has it all—or at least as much as could be put in prose and in English. For it is rarely possible for any one but a poet to translate poetry; and I am not a poet, while of poets Horace has always most successfully defied translation.

T. R. G.

CONTENTS

LECTURE II

§ I

§ II

xiii

xv

xvi

HORACE

I

"To attempt to say anything new about Horace may seem absurd", wrote Henry Nettleship a half century ago; and perhaps it may seem as absurd today, to those who were brought up on Horace. But England today goes after strange gods—graphs and germs and neutrons; even Euclid is dethroned; and in this age of challenge and economics it is perhaps more needful to say the old things about Horace than anything new. Take, then, what I have to say not as a new revelation, but as a simple confession of faith from one of another day, a survivor in a century to which he does not belong.

I

Horace is one of the most autobiographic of all poets; like "the late Elia", his favourite figure was the first person, making himself many or reducing many unto himself. So I am emboldened to be a little autobiographic on my own account—among friends and fellow-citizens, especially as the story begins across the road. A confession of faith involves in any case just a suspicion of egotism, not least when it concerns letters; but out of it comes a real question as to the appeal of a poet, its strength and its sources.

Then let us begin in September 1883, when a rather alarmed boy passed into the Lower Sixth at the Bristol Grammar School, to spend a year under the flashing eye and sharp temper of John George Sowerby Muschamp. One of the works to be read that autumn was the third book of Horace's *Odes*, as edited by Thomas Ethelbert Page. The combination was transforming; Horace, Muschamp and Page turned the boy into an enthusiast for the Classics, a fanatic who has never repented;

and they won for themselves an affection which the years have deepened. Muschamp was not, as I might seem to have suggested and as in 1883 I feared, a *plagosus Orbilius*; but with Horace for a text he worked a conversion. That Christmas vacation with my own money (and I hadn't too much at that time) I bought another of Page's Horace volumes, and read the first book of the *Odes* because I wanted to read it myself. Horace fixed my future; my life was to be spent with the Classics.

Long years afterwards, I taught Latin for five winters in a Canadian University, my second Alma Mater, Queen's College, Kingston, in a scene which Nature and History make a wonder and a delight with vast waters and heroic memories. On my first arrival I found the first three books of the *Aeneid* already set; and we read them together, the class and I; and winter by winter we took the *Aeneid*, three books at a time; till, whatever the successive classes may report, I had read Virgil into my own being. And then came a curious experience. I gave an Honours class an ode of Horace to translate at sight; I picked it without looking at it, from old acquaintance. Perhaps it was *Rectius vives*; but I cannot forget the amazement with which, an old enthusiast for Horace, I read anew with a Virgilian's eyes the old poem. *Tendebantque manus ripae ulterioris amore* was the note in my heart; and here I was reading (it seemed) mere prose in metre. What had happened to me? A little later, perhaps, I had to read *The Art of Poetry* with my class; and the contrast with the *Aeneid* was more painful than ever. *The Art of Poetry?* But the *Aeneid was* poetry; and this wasn't. Others have felt the same; "if we like the *Ars Poetica*", wrote Mr Augustine Birrell, "it is because we enjoy reading Horace". For a long time I was indifferent to my ancient idol, and became so wrapped up in Virgil and Wordsworth, that I am never quite certain which name I have used in speaking of either, and the listeners have to guess which I mean by the context. They were (and are) the two gods of my poetic allegiance.

But in 1919 I had to cross the Atlantic; and, just before I sailed, I picked up on David's bookstall, on the Cambridge marketplace, the neatest little Horace you ever bought for a sixpence. It had belonged to the Harvard scholar, Charles Eliot Norton. It was the luckiest purchase. Since then I have crossed the Atlantic again and again, and never without that little Horace. At the end of each book of the *Odes* is a list of the ships on which I have read it, of trains and islands and mountain places in Canada and in the States, and of old scenes in England too, where I have passed my time with Horace. Generally it has been the *Odes*, sometimes the *Epistles*, much less often the *Satires* or *Epodes*. To the *Odes* I turn again and again. Sometimes it is Muschamp and the old School they bring back; sometimes some odd problem of metre or language starts itself—the use of *atque* (which Muschamp banned and Horace didn't), matters of elision, the question of cheaper or dearer wines, Caecuban or Falernian, the pursuit of some friend of the poet's, or of some favourite idea of his, through the whole volume. Sometimes there is no conscious pursuit of anything, but a tranquil enjoyment of an old happiness, to which many things beside old acquaintance contribute—the exquisite art of rhythm and order, the clear bright speech, the quick and graceful movement of ideas, and the friendly poet who smiles at his reader.

Carlyle and other critics have told us to read books in a spirit of acceptance, without criticism in the first instance, but just acquiescence and enjoyment, till you read yourself into the mind and mood of the writer, see things with his eyes, put his values on them, and live (you might almost say) in him. If you call this a lazy way of reading a poet, do! but it is a very delightful way; and whether it is the *Odes* or the *Aeneid* (for I have been reading that as well again and again in these recent summers), this way of reading brings great contentment to the mind, and sometimes (I hope) something of insight—the slow kind of criticism which isn't in the least brilliant, the kind that in an affectionate way wants to know why I find this poetry so congenial, why it stands so much re-reading, why it wakes such echoes of my own past and of the story of the race.

After that I sometimes turn to the professed critics and receive a series of shocks. It appears that I have missed a great deal in

Horace; that, if I had noticed what I had been reading, and had analysed it, and tracked down its implications, and in short been terribly clever and awake—well, the effect might have been very different. I daresay it would. And then—oh! then, I take up Horace again and read him in my own old way; and, if I said anything to all these clever people, it might be this: "I dare say you are right on every point; there is certainly something wrong here, and here, where you struck your finger on the place; yes, and perhaps you are right in saying that the philosophy of the man won't do; and as for his social ethics, and his religion, and economic principles, and so on —; but I don't mind all that". But I really do mind all those things, you know, in real life; at least I flatter myself that I am not a pagan, nor an Epicurean, nor a bachelor; none of the appalling charges of this kind laid against Horace can be brought against me;

and yet I do enjoy Horace. Then I again
wonder why; I have asked myself that
question a number of times. Is it manner or
matter? Is it his art and grace, or his
friendliness? Are such things enough?
When the invitation came to give the Fry
Lectures, here was a chance to find out why
I like Horace. I have wondered whether
I shall find out; and whether you who may
listen to both lectures will guess why, or
agree with me if you do. But the main
thing is—will you also turn back to the poet
and let him take charge of your leisure for
a little? If this is all too personal, too much
about the lecturer, let me remind you I am
not alone in this craving for Horace. Some
of you will remember the charming story
of the old schoolmaster in Percy Lubbock's
Shades of Eton, and how he took fire at the
ode *Eheu fugaces*. R. L. Stevenson again was
once very ill indeed at Davos. A clergyman
was told that Stevenson wanted to see him;

it was very early morning; he dressed, and rushed through the village to the bedside. The novelist was very ill, but he got out his last request. "For God's sake", he said, "have you a Horace?"

Why do we want him so much?

II

I have read somewhere, or perhaps somebody told me, that Horace is the favourite poet of people who do not care for poetry. There is this to be said for the statement, that Horace was peculiarly the author of our English Eighteenth Century. *Then*, it is generally agreed, there was a dull period in English poetry; the lyric note was lost—unless, as a critic has suggested, you reckon with the writers of hymns. Miss Caroline Goad in 1918 produced a stout volume dealing with Horace in Eighteenth-Century literature. It is to be remarked that he had a small place in the Middle Ages. Chaucer, with all his range in books and learning, seems to have been quite unacquainted with Horace, which strikes one as strange, for they must have been congenial. The Middle Ages in general preferred the *Satires* and *Epistles* to the *Odes*, intelligibly; but "at best", writes Professor C. H. Haskins, "Horace had no such popularity as he has enjoyed in modern times".* But after the Renaissance Horace has a larger place.

When Cervantes discusses *Don Quixote* with his friend in his sore need of introductory sonnets and marginal glosses, the friend suggests that he should write the sonnets himself; he could "father them on Prester John of the Indies"; and then he should gather phrases and scraps of Latin which he knows by heart or can easily find; the first specimen is from "Horace or

* C. H. Haskins, *Renaissance of Twelfth Century*, p. 109.

whoever said it", and the next is still more
authentic, if anonymous—

*Pallida mors aequo pulsat pede pauperum
tabernas
Regumque turres.*

Erasmus learnt all Horace (and Terence)
by heart as a schoolboy. Luther himself has
a strange Horatian echo in a serious passage;
forgiveness is indeed a problem, *nodus Deo
vindice dignus* (cf. *A.P.* 191). Ben Jonson
translated the *Art of Poetry* and some of the
Odes; Drummond of Hawthornden records
how he repeated his version of *Beatus ille*,
"and admired it"—the added clause suggests that Drummond felt as we all feel
about other people's translations of Horace,
which in itself suggests fresh thought as to
our poet's appeal. Robert Burton in the
Anatomy of Melancholy steadily quotes
Horace; Sir Thomas Browne in his most
serious moments turns to him, and Herrick

in his lighter moments. Milton writes sonnets on Petrarch's model, in which Cyriack Skinner may read his Horace again and find himself almost Maecenas.

But, as the *Times* reviewer of Miss Goad's book said, Horace seems in Queen Anne's reign to have burst upon the English world as a new and popular author. The urbanity, the quiet satire, the common-sense view of life, all appealed. Addison, Pope and Johnson are steeped in him. Fielding gave to *The History of Tom Jones* the Horatian motto, *Mores hominum multorum vidit*—cut away in the modern reprints. He inspires the light verse of Prior—"Horace is always in his mind"; William Cowper with his Classical scholarship, his humour, his grace, comes even nearer him; Burke quotes him to the House of Commons in arguing for conciliation with America, and Pitt for the abolition of the slave trade. Praed's verse, all English light verse where touch and wit

13

have play, goes back to Horace. William Makepeace Thackeray is a born Horatian, more Horatian perhaps than he guessed, *anima naturaliter Horatiana*. I opened the *Roundabout Papers* at random the other day for another purpose and I found three Horatian echoes in one opening, two or three words being enough to remind you. It was No. viii. Thackeray's speech is full of Horace, and his heart;—no slight testimony to the worth of Horace. You might say that Horace never lost his seat in Parliament till Gladstone retired and solaced his retirement by translating him. Well, Thackeray is not the fashion of the moment with our modern novelists, nor is Horace. A clerical headmaster has, indeed, lamented that "the philosophy of the average public school product is still fundamentally Horatian". To which *The Times* rejoins that one passage of his doctrine remains steadily ours; *aequam memento*, even if we didn't

14

quote it, was an integral part of our lives in the years of the war. A great old English characteristic—but is it also waning today? If the Horatian echo has dropped out of our talk and writing and out of our thought, perhaps we need not at once congratulate ourselves; let us remember that, when Jack Wilkes censured it as pedantry, Dr Johnson at once rejoined: "No, Sir, it is a good thing; there is a community of mind in it. Classical quotation is the *parole* of literary men all over the world". It is hard to feel sure that Parliament and the press, literature or reviewing, are any the saner for the decline of his influence; extravagance never had a friend in him. Horace belonged to the Augustan age, and perhaps he needs an Augustan age, or something like it, to appreciate him; and that is the last description that will be given of this Twentieth Century. Mark Antony, so far, is much more than Octavian our model, brilliant, disorderly, unstable; and, if Horace hated anything, it was the kind of life, public and private, that Antony affected. The triumphal ode for the battle of Actium is not the only evidence for this.

III

The mention of Antony and Augustus brings us at once to think of the environment of our poet. The influence of his age upon a man of letters is generally significant but commonly it is very hard to assess. Does he realize it himself? Does any one of us realize how obviously stamped with date and place he is? We can see the figures 1850 or 1860 on the great Victorians, large and plain, whether they enjoy their happy spacious period or are afraid of it and want to crawl back to the Middle Ages—as some of us would like to regain the safe and sensible Nineteenth Century. Horace and Virgil are pre-eminently the great

Augustans. Now a crude date or two—the battle of Actium which gave Octavian Caesar the sole rule of the world was fought in 31 B.C.; he took the title Augustus in 27; Horace's *Odes*, the most Augustan of all Augustan products, seem to have been published in 23; and Virgil died in 19, when the Augustan age, the reign of Augustus, was still to last for a generation. It was the Augustan age, and four men made it, Augustus, Maecenas, and our two poets.

But the age that made our poets was very different. Virgil was born in 70 B.C., just at the end of the Sullan epoch, Horace in 65 B.C.; both grew up, as our undergraduates have done, under the shadow of the first series of Civil Wars; both were at the student age when the Senate took to quarrelling with Caesar; they lived through Caesar's wars, and Brutus' wars, and Antony's wars. Both underwent injury of one kind or another; both witnessed hideous wrong done to innocent communities and to society at large; both knew suffering, both had the experience that Seneca later on called "living with beating hearts"— *palpitantibus cordibus vivitur*. So much behind, so much to face here and now, and the future full of hideous doubt—would it be more war, more savagery, the final collapse of city, of country, of society altogether and civilization with it?

> *Damnosa quid non imminuit dies?*
> *Aetas parentum pejor avis tulit*
> *Nos nequiores, mox daturos*
> *Progeniem vitiosiorem.*
>
> (*Odes* iii, 6, 45.)

Fifty years from Sulla's victory to Octavian's, the long uncertainty, the waste of life and work (that Virgil laments), the disappearance of real civil and political government, the rule of the soldier, and fear. Then Augustus and the rule of peace, with its unspeakable relief, which we can understand, the unity of the world, the restoration of law and order, of commerce and agriculture, of family life and religion, the promise made to the human heart that nature and feeling and the deepest things shall be real and valid;—unspeakable change! but would it last? The Emperor's health was always frail; they could not foresee that he would live to seventy-seven; there was always the risk of another traitor Brutus with the foolish knife of the theorist; —and then, what? Could this Golden Age last? When one realizes how everybody asked that question, there shines a new wisdom in Horace's repeated counsel to live today, to take the glad hour that heaven or fortune sends, that comes at any rate, and make the most of happiness while it is there. Of course, you may not like the present government; you may regret the great old days, which Polybius (whom you have not read) described, and to which Cicero looked back so wistfully; you may feel an unreality in this "restored republic", as the Emperor so obtrusively proclaims it; no doubt! but it is government, and not chaos. The horror of chaos is upon these men; so Virgil pleads for a sense of duty and a sense of Rome, and Horace in ode after ode cries: "For God's sake, let us have moderation; *rectius vives*, golden mediocrity, quiet pleasures, and do remember that death is coming anyway". Perhaps (I had not thought of it before; I am not a psychologist) you begin to say to yourselves that this was one of the subconscious influences that took me back to Horace in 1919.

But I spoke just now of the School across the road and of the keen quick Muschamp, and their part in my return to Horace. The nation has its past, and every one of us has his own. It is curious to look back and to find that not what we chiefly noted at the time is the major factor in life; the things that shape us are hardly in our diaries—they didn't count that evening. In spite of all that is said about our remodelling our past, forgetting dates, transposing events, and other lapses of memory, our "Reminiscences" tell the tale better than the diaries; and perhaps the reminiscences that come when we are talking about something else are the best and the most reliable. Now one of the things that people, who notice the obvious, always remark in Horace is his difficulty in keeping to the point; his odes are not in the least like insurance policies; all sorts of things dart into his mind, and in a twinkling (if you allow there is an art in twinkling) there they are on his page; and what connexion the end of an ode (or of an epistle) has with the beginning, the adepts of relevancy can't see for the life of them. Once more I interpolate; that is exactly what most of us like so much about his work; and in among these delightful irrelevancies, come reminiscences, and allusions to the old river Aufidus and the woods, and the father, and the school, and the rest—the very things that made our poet and gave him his charm, and the deeper value that generally underlies charm. Elia's favourite figure, as we saw, was the personal pronoun, and he talks about Mackery End, and my cousin Bridget, and Christ's Hospital, and old china, and his folios, those ragged veterans. So let us go to Venusia, which is very near Mackery End in Hertfordshire.

IV

We know the date of his birth, for providentially a wine jar was "born in the same year, in the consulship of Manlius", that is, in 65 B.C.; and he completed four times eleven years in the December when Lollius and Lepidus were consuls, 21 B.C. Horace leaves us in no doubt as to his early home; he was born on the banks of the Aufidus, a violent river (*Odes* iii, 30, 10), resounding afar (*Odes* iv, 9, 2) and apt to loose the deluge on the cultivated fields (*Odes* iv, 14, 25) and cut away his banks (*Sat.* i, 1, 58). Venusia was the country town, and Daunus was the legendary king (*Odes* iii, 30, 11; iv, 14, 26). There was a doubt—perhaps two; does Bristol belong to Gloucestershire or Somerset? was Horace Lucanian or Apulian?—he asks the question himself (*Sat.* ii, 1, 34). The other doubt is about the quantities he may choose to give to the vowels of Apulia. The family farm was small and lean, and the parent poor (*macro pauper agello, Sat.* i, 6, 71), but, like Virgil's father, he added other means of livelihood to farming, and was an auctioneer or auctioneer's assistant in a small way (*praeco...aut...coactor, Sat.* i, 6, 86). He was a *libertinus*, as people later on reminded his son, a freedman or the son of a freedman, but a Roman citizen, and the poet was freeborn (*ingenuus, Sat.* i, 6, 8). The local society was not exalted; neither father nor son cared for the high and mighty sons of high and mighty centurions (*Sat.* i, 6, 73). The elder Horace, some conjecture, may have been a prisoner of war and come so to slavery for a time, which, if true, might not endear the centurions to him. It is an antiquarian point, but not of supreme interest to the reader today, who by now shares the outlook of Maecenas that the quality of the man is of more account than the precise legal status of his deceased parent.

Cum referre negas quali sit quisque parente
Natus dum ingenuus, persuades hoc tibi vere.
(*Sat.* i, 6, 7; etc.)

Horace never alludes to his other parent; with him, as with Virgil, all the emphasis is on the father. Partly, that is the ancient way; men did not write books or poems about their mothers, who, it is to be feared, had often little to contribute to their sons' minds. Perhaps it is not till we reach St Augustine, that we find a great man profoundly influenced by his mother. It would almost seem that the mother must have dropped out while Horace was still a child; it is the father who takes the boy to Rome. The modern reader may feel in reading some of Horace's earlier work that his tone as to relations with women, with its frequent failure to recognize personality or feeling in them, would be almost impossible for a man who had grown up with mother or sisters. But there modern and ancient differ; women in antiquity probably looked on themselves in a different way from modern women, demanded less of life, and were perhaps not more discontented. It may also be considered that, in the passages recalled, Horace may be deliberately imitating Lucilius, the unfortunate model of his unhappier days.

But enough of fact and accuracy—enough for the moment—let us turn to the poet's reminiscences, which, we agreed, might give us his truer biography. The challenge is quick to reach us; he was a child of miracle, he assures us, *non sine dis animosus infans*; and we shall see how full his life became of amazing theophanies—

> No mere mote's breadth, but teams immense
> With witnessings of Providence.

He strayed, he tells us, from the threshold—no, I would rather have him play with the pronunciation of Apulia, than name the Polly of the nursery or the editor; he strayed up on to Mount Vultur and was lost; and there as he lay, worn out with play and sleep, the wood pigeons of story covered

him with leaves. The sacred laurel and
myrtle kept him safe from vipers and bears
—which, the conscientious student of
Natural History will assure you, do not
normally eat infants, or indeed molest them
unprovoked. But the neighbours in the
surrounding villages wondered, all of them,
at the safety of the marvellous child.

Me fabulosae Vulture in Apulo
Nutricis extra limen Apuliae
  Ludo fatigatumque somno
    Fronde nova puerum palumbes

Texere, mirum quod foret omnibus
Quicumque celsae nidum Acherontiae
  Saltusque Bantinos et arvum
    Pingue tenent humilis Forenti,

Ut tuto ab atris corpore viperis
Dormirem et ursis, ut premerer sacra
  Lauroque collataque myrto,
    Non sine dis animosus infans.

               (Odes iii, 4, 9–20.)

Thus it was ever throughout life; he belongs to the Italian Muses, the *Camenae*; they always guard him, and always would, even if he went to Britain. *Visam Britannos hospitibus feros*; that prophecy is surely abundantly fulfilled; and as surely he has been among the forces that have civilized us (*Odes* iii, 4, 21–36).

But envious tongues in Rome repeated that he was a freedman's son, and we may for once be grateful to human spite. For it stirred him up to write one of his manliest poems, the sixth *Satire* of the first book— here and there satire in our sense, that we may not waste time on Latin lexicography and elaborate what sort of medley *satira* means. Here he tells his story in all seriousness, and—I was going to say, in prose, but it is in hexameters, rather better than his Lucilian imitations; for it is to be remarked in passing that his ear led him in the direction of the Virgilian movement. Let us say, he gives us the plain facts of his career, in a way that must win him respect and affection. The freedman father took the boy to Rome for education of the ampler sort given to the sons of knights and senators, and acted as his footman, escorting him from class to class, a needed safeguard there, as Horace gratefully recalls:

> *Ipse mihi custos incorruptissimus omnes*
> *Circum doctores aderat.*   (*Sat.* i, 6, 81.)

As they walked together, the old man taught him practical morality, using as examples the known characters they met by the way. Good sound morals they were, too—not Christian, of course, nor modern, but fundamentally honest—contentment, uprightness, care for his good name (*Sat.* i, 4, 105); and Horace never lost his sense of what he owed to his father. He would not, he says, have complained if he had put his boy to his own business. (It has been remarked that Horace took a curious, almost un-Roman, interest in trades.*) Instead the father sent the lad to Athens —to the University, as we might by a mild anachronism call it, to the woods of Academe, he says.

Adjecere bonae paulo plus artis Athenae
Scilicet ut vellem curvo dinoscere rectum,
Atque inter silvas Academi quaerere verum.

(*Epp.* ii, 2, 43–45.)

And then the honest old man drops out of the story, probably as most fathers do, by death; but his influence remains, indelible, as the influence of such fathers will.

Then comes a strange episode, stranger as we look into it. On the 15th of March, 44 B.C., Brutus committed the silliest act in Roman history, and murdered Caesar. Into the tangle of events that followed, we need

* Tenney Frank, *Catullus and Horace*, p. 135.

not now go. Brutus played for a while at private life, and "studied" at Athens.* There among others he enlisted Q. Horatius Flaccus, to defend the old order, the privileges of the old nobility and their right to misgovern city and province for their own benefit. The apostle of common sense, as a French critic says, makes his debut as Don Quixote:† what interest had he in politics, in the sham "liberty" of Brutus? What was the freedman's son doing in that galley? Is it better to play Don Quixote in youth or age? Perhaps the debut as Don Quixote explains the apostle of common sense; the experiment sufficed and he returned to his father's ideal of moderation. It is something to be able to say with Horace *Nec lusisse pudet sed non incidere ludum*, or as he did not say *Semel insanivimus omnes*. He

* Rice Holmes, *The Architect of the Roman Empire*, p. 44.
† Edouard Goumy, *Les Latins*, p. 257.

took up arms that were to be no match for the muscles of Caesar Augustus (*Epp.* ii, 2, 48). But how, ask others, came he to be made a military tribune?

Quod mihi pareret legio Romana tribuno.

(Sat. i, 6, 48.)

His fellows asked it, he tells us; and so does posterity. It is like him to half-suggest that the promotion was odd. Young men of high family received the rank as a compliment and promise of higher things; but why Horace? An American scholar thinks we should allow Horace a great deal more practical ability than the poet claims, or indeed wishes us to think he had; it is his way, the way of the urbane universally, to make light of his powers on purpose. Horace had some two years of military service, or, let us say, of actual war, and saw a good deal of Asia Minor and the Balkans. This place and that he saw in a life of utter prose, and he names them again in music—

Laudabunt alii claram Rhodon aut Mitylenen;
(*Odes* i, 7, 1.)

or again

Quid tibi visa Chios, Bullati, notaque Lesbos,
Quid concinna Samos, quid Croesi regia Sardis,
Smyrna quid et Colophon? (*Epp.* i, 11, 1.)

Lovely words, and the genial haze of the past; good humour and the child of the Muses—the two years of the soldier's trade evaporate, and what is left is beauty, and again miracle.

V

Horace was at Philippi. You can read about that battle, which put an end to Roman republicanism, in Shakespeare's *Julius Caesar* (which is largely from Plutarch) or even in the standard historians. I will only quote two passages from the ancients. The last words of Brutus deserve to be recalled, verses he took from some unknown poet:

ὦ τλῆμον ἀρετή, λόγος ἄρ' ἦσθ', ἐγὼ δέ σε
ὡς ἔργον ἤσκουν· σὺ δ' ἄρ' ἐδούλευες τύχῃ.

O hapless Virtue! phrase, mere phrase, thou
    wast,
While I in earnest took thee for a force;
And thou dost prove the veriest toy of
    Chance.*

So Brutus kills himself, with the last re-
proach that the shallow and inconsiderate
always fling at a rational universe which
they have not troubled to understand. But
Horace is our theme. He looks back, and
laughs gently at his army career and his
prowess. The military tribune threw away
his shield, his poor little shield! *non bene*—it
was very inglorious, this act, he says; and
his phrase (as he knows it will) recalls good
Greek precedent; the poets did it, of old,

* The authority for this is Dio Cassius, xlvii, 49.

34

and bought, when necessary, new shields. The shield gone, valour broken, the brave warriors down in the dust, lo! a miracle, amazingly like that Homeric miracle, whereby Poseidon caught away Aeneas (for Virgil and Horace to sing of hereafter) when Achilles son of Peleus came too near slaying him (*Iliad* xx, 325). There are other Homeric precedents of the same kind. "Me," sings Horace, long years afterwards safe in the care of Maecenas, "me, through the midst of the foe, swift Mercury bore me away in a dark cloud, affrighted"—probably more affrighted by the strange experience than by the foe.

> *Tecum Philippos et celerem fugam*
> *Sensi relicta non bene parmula,*
> *Cum fracta virtus, et minaces*
> *Turpe solum tetigere mento.*
> *Sed me per hostes Mercurius celer*
> *Denso paventem sustulit aere.*
>
> (*Odes* ii, 7, 9.)

Or else, as he sings elsewhere (*carmina non prius audita...canto*), he was saved at Philippi, just as he was saved at sea (the Adriatic and the Sicilian wave are named), because he was the friend of the fountains and choirs of the Muses (*Odes* iii, 4, 26). Life, humour and good temper have corrected the blatant Epicureanism of eight and twenty (*Sat.* i, 5, 101; dated 37 B.C.).

Probably after Poseidon rescued him and told him his future, Aeneas went home to supper in Troy, but Homer omits this—*bonus dormitat Homerus* (*A.P.* 359). Prose will keep invading poetry. Mercury lifted Horace clear of flight and foe, we agree; and then, we are told in something like prose, "Philippi sent me back with clipped wings, bereft of my father's home and farm", and it was brazen Poverty that awaited him in Rome.

Dura sed emovere loco me tempora grato,
Civilisque rudem belli tulit aestus in arma

Caesaris Augusti non responsura lacertis.
Unde simul primum me dimisere Philippi
Decisis humilem pennis inopemque paterni
Et laris et fundi, paupertas impulit audax
Ut versus facerem.

(Epp. ii, 2, 46 ff.)

Somehow—his biographer, Suetonius, does not tell us how it was managed; perhaps he was too small to count, and Octavian began to pursue Caesar's policy of mercy—somehow "he was pardoned and bought the position of quaestor's clerk". He was one of thirty-six employed in the treasury with work of some responsibility, with the charge of records, vaults, state moneys, and so forth, and some secretarial duties.* Sometimes the rank of knight came as a reward; and Horace later on, if he really means himself, was made a knight, or at least wore a knight's ring *(Sat.* ii, 7, 53).

* See Tenney Frank, *Catullus and Horace,* p. 147.

Here I am at a loss. He says later on that he had once been what the Victorians called a dandy—careful of the set of his toga and of the neatness of his hair, a very attractive young man (he explains), with a taste for Falernian, of wines not least expensive.

Quem tenues decuere togae nitidique capilli, etc.

(*Epp.* i, 14, 32.)

Does this refer to his student days or to the period of his clerkship?

But he was very much on the ground, as he says, and his wings decisively clipped. It was Poverty that drove him to verse-writing; and very unpleasant verse some of it was. Archilochus and Lucilius were no models for him. "A life," says Dr J. W. Mackail, kindliest of critics, "a life of dull work, tawdry pleasures, and low associates, was turning him into a sort of Dick Swiveller"; and his work shows "coarseness of fibre, bad taste, vulgarity". This is not too severe at all. But, if there were such features in his earlier writing, recognizable too in certain of the *Odes* of better days, there was something else. He captured Varius and Virgil, "whitest of souls" as we all joyfully remember; they saw something in him beyond his actual output, something that developed. Is it worth noting that the sympathies of Virgil and Horace in the Civil War had been on opposite sides? The two poets introduced him to Maecenas, it is thought, about the year 39 B.C. He was tongue-tied and stammered (*infans pudor*) at their first meeting; little was said, and eight months passed before Maecenas sent for him again and "bade him be among his friends" (*Sat.* i, 6, 54–62). Thirty years later, after long friendship, as we all know, Maecenas in his last will addressed the request to Augustus—"be mindful of Horatius Flaccus, as of myself". Statesman and poet died in the same year, 8 B.C.—

as Horace had predicted in the charming astrological ode, *Cur me querellis* (*Odes*
ii, 17).

> *Utrumque nostrum incredibili modo*
> *Consentit astrum.*

This was not all; Augustus wished to
have Horace in closer relation to himself,
and wrote to Maecenas: "He will leave
that parasitic table" (of yours, Maecenas—
an odd phrase) "and come to the kingly
board, and will help me to write my letters".
The phrase may seem indefinite; but everything in Augustus' régime was studiously
indefinite; one Roman citizen could not
exactly pay another to be private secretary,
and Rome long was without a really
organized civil service. It is generally supposed that Augustus offered Horace "ad-
mission to the secrets of state and to a
position of influence at the portal of Imperial favours...to daily companionship

with the inner court circle".* It throws a
new light on the supposed lover of Lydia
and other Greek damsels—a man, it would
seem, though he sought to cloak it, of
experience in army and treasury, master of
an efficient style in Greek and Latin, of
proved tact and integrity. Horace declined
the privilege, and stuck to Maecenas.

> *Jure perhorrui*
> *Late conspicuum tollere verticem,*
> *Maecenas, equitum decus.*
>
> (*Odes*, iii, 16, 18–20.)

The prophet of moderation was satisfied
with moderate prosperity; *satis beatus unicis
Sabinis* (*Odes* ii, 18, 14), *bene est, cui deus
obtulit parca quod satis est manu* (*Odes* iii, 16,
43). He wrote poems for the Emperor at
the Emperor's wish, loyally supported the
régime, and went his own way, now in
town, now in country, busy with Homer

* Tenney Frank, *Catullus and Horace*, p. 210.

and the philosophers, with Greek metres, with quiet friendships and the countryside of Tibur. Prosperity—or perhaps it was friendship—brought out the better elements of his nature. To be on intimate terms with a prime minister—*non ultima laus est*, he says, and quotes a wicked proverb to re-inforce it (*Epp.* i, 17, 35). But it is more than distinction; it is an education for a real man, deepening and widening him.

This point is emphasized by Walter Bagehot in his interesting comparison of Horace and Béranger. For all their resemblance (and geniality is the chief of it— "each knows he is as happy as he can be") they are unlike in their attitude to political liberty; Béranger had a zeal for it which Horace did not share. But "Horace", says Bagehot, "had the almost unequalled felicity of watching the characters and thoughts and tendencies of the governors of the world, the nicest manipulation of the most ingenious statesmen, the inner tastes and predilections which are the origin of the most important transactions" —a great education, indeed, "and yet", he continues, "Horace had the ease and pleasantness of the common and effortless life".*

But friendship with Virgil too must be reckoned as a factor of no less import; all humanism is summed up in Virgil, and his friendship always makes better men of us.

* Dryden suggests something else, in his *Discourse concerning the Origin and Progress of Satire*, speaking of his "acquaintance with Maecenas, and his introduction into the court of Augustus, and the familiarity of that great emperor: which, had he not been well-bred before, had been enough to civilize his conversation, and render him accomplished and knowing in all the arts of complacency and good behaviour; and, in short, an agreeable companion for the retired hours and privacies of a favourite, who was first minister".

Virgil brings Horace, and not too late
in life, to a reasonable and comfortable
prosperity, which is something for any man
and was a great deal for Horace; but he
brings him also into an atmosphere of
friendship, where his gifts are recognized
and valued. The harsh contacts, the
squalours and hardships, of the crippled
life are over; and in rest and peace and
sunshine the man develops and his genius
is seen.

*Hoc erat in votis: modus agri non ita magnus
Hortus ubi et tecto vicinus jugis aquae fons
Et paulum silvae super his foret. Auctius atque
Di melius fecere.*   (*Sat.* ii, 6, 1.)

Did any farm, at Mossgiel or anywhere
else, yield such a crop as that which
"gave Horace to himself" (*Epp.* i, 14, 1)
and to us?

II

II

I

Horace tells us that he once thought of writing Greek verse, but the deified Romulus appeared to him after midnight, when dreams are true, and forbade him;— it was as mad an idea as to carry logs into the forest; the great company of the Greeks was large enough already (*Sat.* i, 10, 31–35). Once more, you see, a theophany in this genial life of miracle and reminiscence. Thenceforth—and, I suspect, previously— he confined himself to Latin. He began with imitations of Archilochus, whom rage had armed with the iambus so peculiarly his own, and of Lucilius. But rage is not the natural note of Horace, and no one wants to read twice the poems which he designs to look like the proper explosion of rage— at least you would hardly read them a second time for pleasure. Good temper is his genius, and time and whitening hair help it: *Lenit albescens animos capillus.* So he outgrows Lucilius as well, after imitating him long enough and too faithfully; he discards the Lucilian themes and the Lucilian haste, and writes (as we saw) hexameters, which, though not Virgilian, show a movement to a rhythm much more like Virgil's, and much pleasanter to read than his early work. There is neither Ovid's eternal monotony of cleverness about them, nor the mechanical brilliance of Lucan, nor the stimulated anger of Juvenal. In spite of his beginnings Horace was very much more of a Roman than any of these men, and very much more (in the long run) what the English call a gentleman. Germans, I learn, have debated where you will find the real Horace. Gruppe says that Horace is himself only in the *Odes*; Lehrs that the real Horace is never found in the *Odes*. It is hard to understand such a judgment as the

48

latter. But really the French are quicker than the Germans at understanding the Latins; the Gauls, as Sainte-Beuve says, early found their way to the Capitol. Probably most English scholars meet the real Horace somewhere or other in every poem attributed to him, hit or miss. "No other writer, ancient or modern", wrote Professor W. Y. Sellar, "seems equally to speak to each individual as a familiar friend." It is surprising how, in spite of the wonderful development that is so obvious in him, all his work hangs together. Here once more he recalls Lamb.

An American scholar raises an interesting question, when he says that "a poet who has not attempted lyric verse until he is thirty-five years of age is obviously not likely to write ardent love lyrics".* This seems to me dogmatic in its chronology; we frankly cannot date all his poems, and

* Tenney Frank, *Catullus and Horace*, p. 193.

some tempt the suggestion that they are early work—notably, I should say, the poem in the fourth book of the *Odes* inviting Virgil to a party and concluding *Dulce est desipere in loco*. Odd words to address to the author of the *Aeneid*; but Charles Lamb, writing to the author of *The Excursion*, a far more solemn work, says: "Now I think I have a wider range in buffoonery than you".* But suppose the *Aeneid* not yet written; suppose the ode taken, as we say, out of a drawer, to help to fill a new volume, a relic and a reminiscence of those early days, when Virgil and Horace were first acquainted, when Virgil could be called "the client of young nobles"—*juvenum nobilium cliens*—(and Horace never outgrew his liking for high company, if it was good); suppose all this, which is almost necessary to explain the ode at all; then

* Letter of 19 September, 1814; Lucas, *Letters of Charles Lamb*, No. 199.

Horace tried his prentice hand long before thirty-five. But, as Plato says, we must not abruptly reject the words of the wise, in case there is after all something in them. So here; for I turn to another writer of a very delightful book, and, in his *Letters to Dead Authors*, I find the same thing put in another way by Andrew Lang. "You sing of women and wine—not all whole-hearted in your praise of them, perhaps, for passion frightens you, and 'tis pleasure more than love that you commend to the young. Lydia and Glycera, and the others, are but passing guests of a heart at ease in itself, and happy enough when their facile reign is ended. You seem to me like a man who welcomes middle age."

A man who welcomes middle age! Is not that how we all think of Horace, once we have put his distressing efforts of youth, those *Epodes* and *Satires*, aside? If the porter at Neaera's door make a fuss about the message, he says to his slave—well, come away; I would not have stood it when Plancus was consul.

> *Dic et argutae properet Neaerae*
> *Murreum nodo cohibere crinem:*
> *Si per invisum mora janitorem*
>   *Fiet, abito.*
> *Lenit albescens animos capillus*
> *Litium et rixae cupidos protervae;*
> *Non ego hoc ferrem calidus juventa*
>   *Consule Planco.*

(Odes iii, 14, 21 ff.)

Consule Planco—that was the year of Philippi, 42 B.C.; and now Augustus is returning conqueror from the Spanish shore; so it must be the end of 25 B.C., says Henry Nettleship, or the beginning of 24 B.C. "All the editors", I read elsewhere, severely criticize the ode, starting as it does with three commonplace stanzas, formal, frigid and official, and ending with licentious vigour—ask Neaera to come, and, if there is any difficulty, never mind her! I am not an editor, and I confess to a very friendly feeling for the ode; who doesn't love the ending *Consule Planco*? And suppose there is just a little humour about the whole thing? Horace has the gift of "thinking of more than one thing at a time" (which W. P. Ker described as the gist of humour) and the habit of laughing at himself.

II

But I must pull myself up; I am running away from my scheme and my notes; and this lecture was to be nothing if not orderly. I meant to deal with the matter and the manner of the poems, and then with the mind behind them; and I seem to have got them mixed. Well, mixed they are in Horace, and he either does not scheme his poems very clearly, or he abandons his scheme, or perhaps his art is to be artless.

People have suggested that. I will give you one or two schemes of the *Odes* in a few minutes, and then go on doucely with my own, unless Horace tempts me to digress. But there is another thing I want to say first, which doesn't quite fit into the scheme; I hope you will forgive it.

Horace, if you will let me put it so, seems to me to be the Boswell of the Augustan age. You will ask at once—then, who is the Johnson? I have to own, there is not one, not even Maecenas—"his Mrs Harris of a Maecenas", as a Bristolian college friend of mine irreverently wrote in his youth, before he was a Fellow of the British Academy. The Boswell of the age— who really tells us most of what we know about it; for Virgil writes of a remote past and of all time, Roman through and through, and his theme allows no gossip. There are historians, of course, but they are not contemporary; few of us read them;

and for the real warp and woof of the period we rest on Horace. I find the critics this time are with me. Thus Wight Duff says, "we meet the actual flesh and blood of the new Rome in Horace"; Goumy, that he takes us about in Roman society, leaving us the impression of having been among people of *esprit*, very polished, full of an amiable scepticism, an *élite* of very cultured and elegant experts in life; Patin that he gives us the living expression of his day, and of the best of it. "What a position Horace has", wrote G. F. Watts to Gladstone; "I have often wondered at it, and conclude it is owing to something apart from literary excellence. I think it is that through all the poetry the man of his age is speaking, seldom echoing the thoughts of other men and other times". If you try to count the names of his friends, to whom he wrote his *Odes* and *Epistles*, you will think again of Boswell; it is only in the books of these two men that we know, most of us, even the names of their contemporaries (indebted thus to men of letters they did not admire, *quem rodunt omnes*); let alone the ideas, tastes, humours, follies and philosophy of those formative times. There is also more of the public history of the reign (if the word is allowed) than a general impression of the poems might suggest. Horace is one of those writers like Herodotus who tell you more than you notice. But this point should have attention later on.

III

Dryden has his classification of the *Odes*: "Some of them are panegyrical, others moral, the rest jovial, or (if I may so call them) Bacchanalian". M. Patin's grouping expands this a little. Let us take the French scholar's scheme, for it brings out a point of importance scarcely felt in Dryden's.

First, then, M. Patin sets odes political

and religious, giving, as we have just suggested, a history of the Emperor's achievements in war and peace, and a gallery of political figures. Augustus is long ago; his reign is in the distant past; and it is arguable that the historical value of poetry is very different from its poetic significance. The English reader has a certain right to ignore the Spanish campaigns, the standards restored by the Parthians, the alleged impression made upon Indians and Britons on the outer edges of the world; but for the Roman reader they meant practical politics. Never over-done, never over-emphasized, just broached and (as it were) run away from, there is always a hint, a counsel, in these references, a plea for acceptance, for reason, and for peace—a very genuine public service, the more valuable for the light touch, the fugitive reminder. It is debated how far the poet was ever a thorough-going

Caesarian; he says more and less than Virgil; he will never quite surrender to Augustus, but he recognizes him, and in many odes, quite apart from the odes of command in the fourth book which celebrate the Imperial victories of Tiberius and Drusus, there is a clear vindication of the real work of Augustus for the state. But it is not propaganda; oh dear no! go and ask Neaera, or—better still (for who would wish, as Dr Johnson put it, for "a set of wretched *un-idea'd* girls"?*) ask Maecenas to a very quiet party—no shouting!† *Dona praesentis cape laetus horae et linque severa* (*Odes* iii, 8, 27). The odes to Maecenas are among the pleasantest of all, which is

* Boswell's *Johnson* (Birkbeck Hill), vol. i, p. 251.
† *Procul omnis esto Clamor et ira.* I would like to remind such readers as will not believe that it is *the* Virgil to whom *Odes* iv, 12, is inscribed, because of references to *lucrum* and patrons, that this deprecation of shouting is addressed to a Prime Minister.

significant, for that was his pleasantest friendship; and this brings us at once to our next group.

M. Patin sets next the odes of friendship —a class which surely overlaps the rest and includes nearly all Horace's work; for friendship is the keynote of most of it. It would be curious to discuss how far self-revelation and self-effacement make friendship; they are both in Horace's poetry. His friends shall smile with him—sometimes, if they like, at the "fat and trim little man" (the Emperor himself chaffed him on being so short and round) "with his well-cared-for skin, a pig of Epicurus' herd".

Me pinguem et nitidum bene curata cute vises,
Cum ridere voles, Epicuri de grege porcum.

(*Epp.* i, 4, 15,16.)

"A man of small frame", he says else-where, "early white-haired, rather fond of the sunshine, quick-tempered but the sort to be easily reconciled,—and forty-four."

Corporis exigui, praecanum, solibus aptum,
Irasci celerem, tamen ut placabilis essem.

(*Epp.* i, 20, 24.)

His friends may laugh gently at his running away at Philippi, tossing his shield from him—but, by the way, doesn't that some-how suggest the "forgive and forget" policy of the Caesars? And his prospective transformation into a swan (*Odes* ii, 20)—

Album mutor in alitem
Superne nascunturque leves
Per digitos humerosque plumae.

"Furchtbare Realität", said Goethe; there's no real poetry in the *Odes*, Goethe added, not in his most inspired mood; the great can be far too impressive. But Horace did not want to be impressive to his friends—

for various reasons; partly, he was subtler than that, and, then, they really were friends. He tells them once and again of his deadly peril on the Sabine estate that Maecenas gave him, when the bough so nearly crashed on his head—some bandit must have planted the tree, a parricide and a poisoner, no doubt of it.

> *Illum et parentis crediderim sui*
> *Fregisse cervicem et penetralia*
> *Sparsisse nocturno cruore*
> *Hospitis; ille venena Colcha*
>
> *Et quidquid usquam concipitur nefas*
> *Tractavit, agro qui statuit meo*
> *Te triste lignum, te caducum*
> *In domini caput immerentis.*
>
> (*Odes* ii, 13, 5–12.)

But once more a theophany, as so often. Faunus this time, himself in person, with his right hand, Faunus the guardian of men

whom Mercury loves—you remember?—
turned the guilty log aside.

> *Me truncus illapsus cerebro*
> *   Sustulerat, nisi Faunus ictum*
> *Dextra levasset, Mercurialium*
> *Custos virorum.*
>
> (*Odes* ii, 17, 27.)

And Bacchus too seems to have had a hand
in the rescue (*Odes* iii, 8, 7). But how nearly
Horace passed into the most literary and
most charming of other worlds! How near
he came to seeing Proserpine and Aeacus,

> *Quam paene furvae regna Proserpinae*
> *Et judicantem vidimus Aeacum*
> *   Sedesque discretas piorum,*
>
> (*Odes* ii, 13, 21.)

and of course the Greek poets, whom—but
it is another ode that tells how one born by
the Aufidus brought the Aeolian song to
Italy and merited the Delphic crown of the

Muse (*Odes* iii, 30). He claims no original genius, only the minor credit of an adapter. A friend, with a sense of humour and something of aptitude for friendship, can come very near Horace in these *Odes* and *Epistles*; and still he keeps something to himself, one feels. "With this same key Shakespeare unlocked his heart?" asks Browning. Well, some of it!

The third group of odes M. Patin labels "gallant and Bacchic". Some modern critic touched off Ovid's most famous work as "the Art of Love—without love". The Greek damsels of Horace's odes need not detain us. The schoolboy, who could not find in his English-Latin dictionary a Latin word for "drawing room", was touching, little as he guessed it, the real weak spot of ancient civilization; there was no meeting place, and little meeting, for men and women of equal station in society. But as no one, I suppose, would try to find

Claribel and Mariana and the other beautiful creatures with lovely names, whom Tennyson sang, in the census returns of the early Victorians, we need not ask for Lydia's postal address, though in case of need Greek literature might find her. Let us remember Lyde, rather; there are three of her; but I mean the charming one "ower young to marry yet". Mercury himself, the god of the rescue at Philippi, the teacher of Amphion, is mobilized to win her ears, she is so obstinate and young; Mercury, who can set woods moving and halt rivers, who can prevail with tigers and much more terrible creatures; just think how he played his lyre in Hades, and the daughters of Danaus—and lo and behold! Lyde, for whom the tale is to be told, drops out of her poet's mind, and he tells the tale of Danaus' daughters himself, inimitably. But you would hardly call it a love-poem. Would Lyde? Then as to Bacchus, there is the

64

riotous call to drink and scatter the roses—
in winter-time, too ("Paelignian cold"), as
A. W. Verrall, barrister-at-law, carefully
noted, perhaps forgetful for once of
humour and exaggeration, which in other
capacities he enjoyed; it was to be a very
wasteful party indeed, with Murena at it
(iii, 19), as bad as the Lamia frolic, where
Damalis indulges so violently (i, 36). But
once again, a theophany—Horace one day
surprised Bacchus himself among the lonely
hills, with an audience of listening nymphs
and quite genuine satyrs:

> *Bacchum in remotis carmina rupibus*
> *Vidi docentem, credite posteri,*
>   *Nymphasque discentes et aures*
>   *Capripedum Satyrorum acutas;*
>
>   (*Odes* ii, 19.)

and he was inspired there and then, with
the most literary of Bacchic exaltations, to
write an ode in exquisite metre, with only

two elisions, and abundance of legend and myth in its thirty-two lines. Few dithyrambs could imply more essential sobriety. The parties sound very dreadful; probably enough Horace had known them (with less suggestion of Greek literature) in the Dick Swiveller days, but his real taste was for a very different kind of entertainment, on the Sabine farm, where the talk would have a tinge of philosophy, of the practical kind, not far removed from the old lessons of the poet's father; and old neighbour Cervius would clinch things with an old wives' tale—the fable, for instance, of the town and the country mouse, which Horace tells again with plenty of character and movement, and in charming metre (*Sat.* ii, 6).

The fourth class consists of "moral odes", and there are plenty of them and this class again overlaps the others. Take the great six Alcaic odes of the third book, and decide in which group you will place them. Do they belong in this category of "moral odes" or are they, taken together, as great and signal a service rendered to the State as citizen could hope to achieve—the *Aeneid* only excepted? Is this language too high? Or is it not true that every state rests on ideas, and that here Horace sets forth in immortal lines the very ideas on which Augustus would have the Empire rest? *Delicta majorum* is a plea for piety, an ode neither Epicurean nor playful, but grave and serious, with some real conviction behind it; surprising to the careless reader. It is tempting to suppose that there might have been fewer of the "gallant and bacchic" type, if the poet had not wished to "vary the emotional effect". For, like R. L. Stevenson, descendant of that Smith whom Burns heard "open out his cauld harangues", Horace is a born moralist, a maker of proverbs, a lover of apologue and aphorism —*dimidium facti qui coepit habet: sapere aude*

(*Epp.* i, 2, 40). Country mouse and canny fox, Homer and Aristippus, are always reinforcing his lessons in practical wisdom. He can lapse at times into the sententious. He might have been a Scotsman and a Calvinist, "if", as a colleague of mine, at once English and Anglican, puts it, "he had not fortunately been a heathen". (My ideas of good fortune are hereditarily different.) But, my colleague continues, Horace saw things so profound that they now appear obvious; and if experience could ever be taught, Horace is the man to teach it; for, he adds, "it isn't only Poetry, when your feelings begin to kick; a landscape doesn't kick". Nor do Horace's *Odes* or his *Epistles*, and in this world it is a great thing to find something that doesn't kick. Poetry has been defined by Wordsworth as emotion re-collected in tranquillity. Horace's tranquillity is so overmastering that some readers suspect there

68

was very little emotion—which is what he wished. It is only to Maecenas, and perhaps Virgil, that he wishes to disclose real feeling. *Nil admirari*; but do you believe it? He is not really a philosopher, much as he likes to dabble in philosophy, to play at Epicureanism and to make fun of the Stoics. The ode *O diva gratum* (i, 35) could never have been written by a philosopher. Why, he has Chance and Predestination and the fear of the gods hopelessly tangled. It is worse than Virgil's Silenus idyll. But neither could any of the other odes have been written by a philosopher.

Professor A. Y. Campbell, of Liverpool, sets out carefully the constituents that go to a Horatian ode, with the premise that out of the multiplicity comes a real unity. *Recipe*, he almost says, first, a deliberately literary quality, a strong suggestion of the greater and older Greeks. (Horace despised the Alexandrines, as a matter of fact—a

69

very significant antipathy; they posed, they displayed their art, and paraded their obscurity—no poets for a man with a sense of humour.) Next, continues Mr Campbell, add the occasion, actual or imaginary, the weather (*Vides ut alta*, and a rare occasion it is, we are told, to see Soracte snowclad), a feast, an anniversary. And the person to whom it is addressed—as Mercury, eloquent grandson of Atlas or Maecenas of Etruscan kings. After this, the moral, mythical and national elements, with a flavour (not too strong, but quite recognizable) of the poet himself. Mr Campbell's *recipe* is admirable; but, lest you quote it later about me, I will do it first about him. Isn't all such analysis a little like Olivia's account of herself in *Twelfth Night*? "I will give out divers schedules of my beauty; it shall be inventoried, and every particle and utensil labelled to my will: as, item, two lips, indifferent red; item, two grey eyes, with lids to them; item, one neck, one chin, and so forth". Of course, you had to see the real Olivia—*totum illud formosa*; Mr Campbell said as much, the ode of Horace has a unity of its own and you have to read the ode. Which said, I turn to analysis again, for I am not going to read any ode to you to-day. Some of you would want it in English, and the odes have wrecked the reputations of endless translators; and I am cannier, *renuit negitatque Sabellus*. You will take it as a tribute to Horace that none of us can quite do the thing again in English.

IV

It is remarked how limited a range of themes we find in Horace, *Odes* or *Epistles*; and how often his ideas recur, and yet with what variety of turn and phrase. The tastes of men vary;—here let me interpolate a line or two from William Cowper—"Horace", he wrote to Joseph Hill in 1769, "observing this difference of temper in different persons, cried out a good many years ago in the true spirit of poetry, 'How much one man differs from another!' This does not seem a very sublime exclamation in English, but I remember we were taught to admire it in the original". To continue: human hopes are frustrated; danger threatens from unexpected quarters (who could have thought that a tree on the beloved farm would so nearly kill Horace? *quid quisque vitet nunquam homini satis cautum est in horas, Odes* ii, 13, 13); and death is inevitable. It seems a gloomy series of ideas, but somehow the poetry that embodies it is not gloomy.

Ire tamen restat Numa quo devenit et Ancus —so in the *Epistles* (i, 6, 27); *tamen* none the less, though you are the famous figure in the colonnade of Agrippa and on the Appian Way. And beyond is nothing— *mors ultima linea rerum est* (*Epp.* i, 16, 79).

So too in the charming ode that greets the spring with its *Diffugere nives* (Thackeray's "diffugient snows"), spring with its grasses and leaves, its dances of Graces and Nymphs; the year bids frame no eternal hopes (*immortalia ne speres, monet annus*); all is change and cycle—

Nos ubi decidimus
Quo pater Aeneas, quo dives Tullus et Ancus,
Pulvis et umbra sumus.   (*Odes* iv, 7.)

So in that other ode, as exquisite, *Solvitur acris hiems* (i, 4). Nothing can avail to change the common destiny, not the sceptred race, nor the eloquence of Torquatus, nor the music of Virgil (*Odes* i, 24, 13), nor the science of Archytas (*sed omnes una manet nox et calcanda semel via leti, Odes* i, 28, 15), nor sacrifice, nor offering, nothing; and so it ever was; Ancus, Antilochus, Pirithous, all human story is the same. *Moriture Delli*, is his address to one friend,

73

to be in the end *victima nil miserantis Orci* (*Odes* ii, 3). What then? *Durum, sed levius fit patientia!* (*Odes* i, 24, 19).

The facing of the inevitable—it runs through the poets, from Homer and the great words of Sarpedon to Glaucus, ὦ πέπον εἰ μὲν δὴ... "Friend of my soul, were it that, once thou and I were escaped from *this* war, we should live for ever free from age and death, neither would I fight among the foremost nor would I send thee into the battle that gives men renown. But now— for, none the less, fates of death stand over us, aye! ten thousand of them, which mortal man may not fly nor escape, let us go, whether we shall yield glory to another, or another to us" (*Iliad* xii, 322–328); to Virgil

Stat sua cuique dies, breve et irreparabile tempus Omnibus est vitae   (*Aeneid* x, 467);

and to Wordsworth with his "frequent sights of what is to be borne". The inevitable

74

—and the wars are over that bring men renown (poor mankind, and sad renown by now!); yet though much is taken, much remains—spring and the trees, the cup (if you care for it), and pleasure (if you are young), and always friendship, and patience. The ship will sink, no doubt, but we can walk the deck together, and talk over the past—*O saepe mecum tempus in ultimum deducte*, what days we had together, Pompeius, happy days of nard and wine, and dreadful days, too, *tecum Philippos*; and now you are at my side again, and that means a happy day (*Odes* ii, 7). A sad happiness, you will say, "a melancholy satisfaction" as our grandparents put it—

> Sad Patience, too near neighbour of
>   Despair.

But if the cup and the company at times seem frivolous enough, it is not unmanly, this facing of death.

Readers have debated whether Horace really loved the countryside, or was its *ami assez tiède*, as a friendly Frenchman put it. He was not Wordsworth, of course; but there are different ways of loving the country. If he tells us that he is fickle, sighs for Tibur when he is in Rome and then wishes himself back, there are two things to remember. Horatius Flaccus and Charles Lamb are very candid about their failings. Horace's *ego* sometimes means *you*. It is a stroke of genius to confess your own faults to mend another's; and Horace does it freely—he is never better than his company, but somehow his company is better for him. And then I cannot understand any one reading his exquisite pictures of Tibur and the water and the country place:

> *domus Albuneae resonantis*
> *Et praeceps Anio ac Tiburni lucus et uda*
> *Mobilibus pomaria rivis*
>
> (*Odes* i, 7, 12),

or again

> *Tibur Argeo positum colono*
> *Sit meae sedes utinam senectae*
> > *(Odes* ii, 6, 5),

and not realizing there is real feeling here
as in Virgil's

> *Praeruptis oppida saxis*
> *Fluminaque antiquos subterlabentia muros.*

Horace, as I have said already more than
once and mean to say again, will always
understate a feeling, like the Englishman.
A friendly critic notes "the vein of half
ironic philosophizing which flavours so
happily the rural enthusiasms of Horace".*

Of course, he liked the town too—to
potter about, on foot and alone, through
the market. He asks the price of kitchen
stuff and grain; he strolls about the Circus
and the Forum as evening falls. He listens
to the fortune-tellers. And then he saunters

* Herford and Simpson, *Ben Jonson*, vol. ii, p. 369.

77

homeward to a quite vegetarian supper, tidy but without luxury. "And so to bed." And next morning he lies abed, with his book or his manuscript, till he thinks he will rise (*Sat.* i, 6, 111–128). Town has its pleasures, but they seem innocent enough, and quite consistent with enjoyment of the farm as well.

Side by side with friendship he finds great satisfaction in books. He reads his Homer over again in the country, at Praeneste, and finds him better than "those budge doctors of the Stoick fur" (*Epp.* i, 2) —and most of us will agree with him. But he obviously read the philosophers too, in some form or other, if not the books of Crantor and Chrysippus, at least their disciples,* or he could not make fun of them so admirably; nor could he do it if he did not care for them. He swears allegiance to none of them, but gives them all a turn

* Cf. *Odes* i, 29, 14.

(*Epp.* i, 1, 13 ff.). Some people can't see how humour and affection can live together, how you can laugh at yourself for your enthusiasms, and make fun of your beliefs, and like them the better, as you do with the friends of whom you can make fun. Homer, and philosophy, and the myths of the Greeks, and the legends of Rome—there is a lot in life after all; and to repeat what is already said (one may be Horatian so far), he is a thorough Roman, proud in our English way of his state, anxious about it, fond of it, and wouldn't for the world be seen waving a silly flag—only, can't you see that the state needs your thought and life? He will not speak of serving the state, as Cicero does in *The Dream of Scipio*; there is no paradise beyond the Milky Way for him; and he doesn't argue with himself about it like Marcus Aurelius; only, can't you see? He *feels*; and, as a critic says, he is more Roman than Maecenas. The great

79

Regulus ode could only have been written by a Roman———.

This is really getting too pathetic and too solemn—*quid fles, Asterie?* What a lot of charming things, flowers and trees, woods and waters (*lucos amoenae quos et aquae subeunt et aurae* (*Odes* iii, 4, 7)), books and poems, jolly legends, long beautiful Greek names (and some Latin), there are in the world—*Venafranos in agros aut Lacedae-monium Tarentum! Non hoc jocosae conveniet lyrae* (*Odes* iii, 3, 69); the Muse mustn't preach; and he is right; Juno has delivered a terrible sermon, weary, dreary, as all the mythological speeches which Horace puts in his odes, in imitation of Pindar. *Prome reconditum, Lyde, strenua Caecubum* (*Odes* iii, 28, 2). This is the third Lyde, the one who can sing, and he tells her to sing. Perhaps some of us like him the better for disguising his feelings, like his Regulus leaving Rome —*atqui sciebat.*

When we turn to consider the manner of
Horace's writing, we have some famous
ancient judgments before us. The phrase of
Petronius comes first, *Horatii curiosa felicitas*,
"which", says Dryden, "I suppose he had
from the *feliciter audere* of Horace himself".*
English cannot be quite so brief. Felicity
we can understand, the happy touch, but
there is good fortune in it; luck is always
with Horace; yes—but care, infinite care,
caution, thought, the trained ear, precision,
and then the inspiration, to use a word not
used by Petronius. Some Greek poet has
the same idea of poetry—

τύχη τέχνην ἔστερξε καὶ τέχνη τύχην.

Art has loved Chance, and Chance loved Art,
Each takes in turn the other's part.
"Of our lyric poets," wrote Quintilian,†

* He refers to *Epp.* ii, 1, 166, *feliciter audet*; cf.
Quintilian's words in the text.

† Quintilian, x, 1, 96.

"Horace is almost the only one who deserves to be read; for he rises at times, and is full of pleasantness and charm; there is variety in his figures, and his boldness in the use of words is most happy (*felicissime audax*)." "The cunning Horace! he can strike his finger on the place, touch one after another of your weaknesses, and he keeps his friend smiling all the time. You let him in, and he plays about your heart; and he is clever at tossing up his nose and catching the public on it" (i, 116). So Persius; "he means", says Dryden "those little vices which we call follies, the defects of human understanding, the peccadillos of life rather than the tragical vices".

Horace's own *aurea mediocritas* is often quoted of his style, his comparison of himself to the Matine bee, so busy with its little tasks, so unlike the torrential Pindar (*Odes* iv, 2); he has to put such a lot of work into so small a product. You see, he hints, it isn't exactly genius; it is only the art, the dexterity that sets the right words together —*tantum series juncturaque pollet* (*A.P.* 242). Of course, he borrowed his metres; it is his pride that he did—that he naturalized Alcaeus and Sappho in Latium. But he says nothing of the amazing instinct for sound and rhythm, which is almost as miraculous in him as in Virgil. There is a strange charm in Alcaics and Sapphics—at least when Horace writes them—something in the metre itself reinforcing the language and the thought. A classical man of my acquaintance has told me that he "feels a sort of almost physical pleasure" in the very construction of Cicero's prose—its movement, its pattern and its cadences. William Wordsworth, in the Preface to *Lyrical Ballads* (1800), speaks of "small but continual and regular impulses of pleasurable surprise from the metrical arrangement" as a real part of the appeal of poetry.

83 6-2

So indeed I feel with the Alcaics and Sapphics above the other metres, delightful as some of them can be. Only one I dislike, and I half think Horace did too, for he only used it once in an ode that I have never heard praised or quoted—*Lydia, dic per omnes*. But *Tyrrhena regum progenies, tibi*—no wonder that that ode is praised, and its metre, susceptible as it is of carrying the gravest and gayest of themes and of blending them.

As to the language, one critic after another notes a prose-like particle—*ergo, quodsi, quatenus*—prose words and colourless, and sometimes such ugly words, calling a spade worse than a spade*—the other Lyde, for instance (*Odes* ii, 11, 21). He is as bad as Wordsworth and Euripides for using "the language actually employed by men". But Horace is sometimes ahead of

* Teuffel, *Latin Literature* (Eng. tr.), vol. i, p. 465, § 6.

his critics, and if they note this use of common words, so did he: *tantum de medio sumptis accedit honoris* (*A.P.* 243). His vocabulary, too, is noted as a short one, which he uses to the full. Dryden will have it that "his words are chosen with as much exactness as Virgil's; but there seems to be a greater spirit in them": and Dryden had some acquaintance with Virgil. But in the criticism of poetry, it is not so much the poet's words that signify as what he does with them; the more commonplace the words, the more wonderful the magic, as readers of Wordsworth know. The most prosaic word may be the making of the poem—*Ergo Quintilium perpetuus sopor* (*Odes* i, 24, 5). Of all things, says Suetonius, obscurity is least of all his fault. The passion of the Alexandrine for the abstruse, the mannered, the allusive, for brute learning, infinite length, and involved diction, he abhors with all other affectations. He is a

85

master of phrase—how many has he coined that we remember? *Consule Planco, splendide mendax, in medias res, nil desperandum, laudator temporis acti*—so many indeed that one may perhaps pause to say that some famous lines are not his, neither *Quem deus vult perdere dementat prius*, nor *Semel insanivimus omnes*, nor *Incidis in Scyllam cupiens vitare Charybdim*. The reader of Boswell does not need this reminder. But to coin a phrase that will stick calls for both art and luck; and Horace, as we saw, had both. An artist in phrase.

Critics have compared his best work to mosaic. The comparison is intelligible, but it does not suggest the movement that one feels in his *Odes*. They have spoken of a certain "economy" in his handling of language; it has even been called "parsi- mony", by a sympathetic critic. *Artis poeticae est*, says Servius, *non omnia dicere*. Horace dislikes all over-expression, all that is high-stepping or exaggerative; it was he who gave us the phrase "purple patch", and no one was shrewder in avoiding the purple patch than himself. Over-loading and over-colouring are always dangers; but Horace avoids them by instinct—an instinct developed by long intimacy with the best models and quickened by the sense of humour. It has been said, to take a parallel from modern times, that the American conception of humour is over-statement, the English under-statement, and that the American consequently is uneasy where irony has play. There Horace is with us; indeed we may well have been influenced by him in this direction in that great Eighteenth Century when he inspired our men of letters. He is, as I have said already in his words or mine, the ideal type of the urbane, making light of what he does:

> *Urbani parcentis viribus atque*
> *Extenuantis eas consulto.*

> (*Sat.* i, 10, 13.)

Avoidance of display and tireless revision are his canons. *Saepe stylum vertas*—"the greatest of all arts, the art to blot"—is his characteristic counsel, even if you have to delay publication "till the ninth year". The poet must cut everything possible away; he must ruthlessly sacrifice to achieve perfection. Ovid is his foil: "Seneca's censure", wrote Dryden, "will stand good against him; *Nescivit quod bene cessit relinquere*: he never knew how to give over when he had done well". Horace did know—none better. The engineer, Henry Maudsley, had certain rules for his profession; when you build an engine or machine, reduce, cut away every pound of weight that you safely can; have nothing that is not definitely working or stabilizing; and simplify. The advice is curiously like Horace's advice to men of letters. His *Art of Poetry* is not in itself very poetic; throughout the more obvious emphasis is on rule, tradition, conventions. He is not so much writing a poem himself as laying down the lines on which Poetry must be made. To be safe, the railway train must run on its lines, and something of the kind is true about Poetry. Plate-laying, of course, is not engine-driving, and sleepers are no substitute for steam. Pindar, if you believe Horace, did without railway lines—*numerisque fertur lege solutis*; Pindar is the most uncompromising champion of steam, to keep up our metaphor, of inspiration; the poet's art cannot be acquired, it can neither be taught nor learnt; it is God-given. But Horace addresses himself to another age, and of inspiration he talks less—unless, of course, when he laughs about the Camenae, when he is so obviously far from serious, he is serious after all and only laughs because he feels, and—because you should never overstate. *Quanto rectius hic qui nil* *molitur inepte* (*A.P.* 140), we might quote of its author.*

He plays with the things he likes best, as he does with others; he minimizes his own gift, boasts of being second hand, puts beauty on a grim fact (as in those wonderful lines about the last goal of Numa and Ancus, and the rest), runs away from the expression of real feeling, fills his own story with miracles that make you smile, weaves myth and astrology in among his warmest expressions of affection, till—till nobody can understand him who doesn't love him, and everybody who loves him does; and that is exactly what he wanted, and what any one else would want, who had the wit to do it. And as for other readers—

Why, other readers find him very improper (as I have admitted he was in his pre-Virgilian days); they tell us he is

* *Recte* and *rectius* seem to be favourite words with Horace.

90

wanting in depth and seriousness, quite without passion for woman, god or humanity, without programme, illumination, idealism, nothing but common sense and Epicureanism. A terrible indictment! but I hope I have given you some grounds at least for bringing in a kindlier verdict. I don't think all that can be quite true about a man who had such gifts of friendship, who was so lovable and has been so loved.

VI

A chance co-incidence of phrase suggests a comparison. Some one has, I think, called the Diary of Marcus Aurelius the breviary of Agnosticism. It is the record of a great man, but a lonely and unhappy man, without friends, alone in his Stoic *cosmos*. The book, of course, was never meant to be read straight through, if it was ever meant to be read by us at all—a book of jottings, notes and reflections, desperately sad and depressing. Dr J. W. Mackail has said that Horace has given us "a secular psalter, for daily and yearly and age-long use". A breviary and a psalter—.

There is doubt and uncertainty in the minds of both men. Marcus is never sure about any future life; there may be one, there may not. Horace is sure there is not, —as sure as Omar Khayyam or Borrow's Mr Petulengro. The ideal of Marcus is avowedly duty—but without any conviction that the doing of duty will produce any result whatever. Horace's ideal— Horace does not talk about ideals; if you read him carelessly, it looks as if his ideal were pleasure, a refined Epicureanism. But, as we have seen, he is Roman too; he thinks of the state—in the stirring times when he plays Don Quixote, and his quieter days on the Sabine farm. Marcus lives a life of question and self-torture; Horace's philosophy is more practical—acceptance of

what comes, and a happy use of it. Mr Lubbock's old schoolmaster "likes to join with an old friend, old popular Horace, in a plaintive strain (*Eheu, fugaces*) that *he* didn't intend very seriously; for these regrets and laments, they belong to the smooth philosophy of an honest poet, comfortable enough in his worldly wisdom— and a companionable old poet too, so life-seasoned, so familiar". Horace is for contentment, for the conditions given—in virtue of a happier temperament, a genius for friendship and unobtrusive happiness.*
Laetus is his word (how alien to Marcus!). That note comes over and over again— *laetus in praesens animus* (*Odes* ii, 16, 25); *dona praesentis cape laetus horae* (*Odes* iii, 8, 27);

* A reference may be forgiven to John Stuart Mill's remarkable tribute to Wordsworth (in his *Autobiography*, pp. 146–150) who had taught him to find an unexpected happiness, real and permanent, which all could share, in Nature. A parallel is, of course, not an identity.

93

laetus sorte tua vives sapienter (*Epp.* i, 10, 44). And some kind of gratitude, too—not a common Roman note, nor very common elsewhere—*tu quamcumque deus tibi fortunaverit horam grata sume manu* (*Epp.* i, 11, 22). Perhaps this also explains why one likes to read him. "Not a profound searching of the mysteries of heaven and earth", says an American scholar,* "but the most satisfactory sort of human living ever yet devised." We have, of course, to search the mysteries, but there are moments, oftener than we sometimes realize, when it is wiser to take the obvious happiness that all may enjoy. What says Borrow's gypsy? "There's night and day, brother, both sweet things; sun, moon, and stars, brother, all sweet things; there's likewise a wind on the heath, brother!"

There is in one of Cicero's later letters to Atticus a cry from the heart, which

* E. K. Rand, *Founders of the Middle Ages*, p. 253.

often comes back to me. "I think I must read my *De Senectute* oftener, the book I sent you. For old age is making me more bitter—I get cross about everything—*stomachor omnia. Sed mihi quidem* βεβίωται. *Viderint juvenes*" (xiv. 21, 3). Yes, I know; *stomachor omnia*—and then the *Odes* bring me back to boyhood, to old friends and good temper. I think I will read them again.

POSTSCRIPT

Frui paratis et valido mihi,
Latoe, dones at precor integra
Cum mente nec turpem senectam
Degere nec cithara carentem.